FROM IDEA TO IMPACT

Ignite Your Creative Entrepreneur

Kingsley Eleweke

Toptoria Development Series

From Idea to Impact: Ignite Your Creative Entrepreneur

By Kingsley David

Be sure to stay up to date with all of our newest series, as well as ways to create passive income by visiting our website here www.toptoria.com

Disclaimer

Kingsley David © 2023– All Rights Reserved

CONTENTS

INTRODUCTION

In a world driven by innovation and ideas, the path to transformation lies in entrepreneurship. It is a path illuminated by the sparks of creativity and the unwavering belief in the power of one's ideas. This book, "From Idea to Impact: Ignite Your Creative Entrepreneur," is a guide that invites you to embark on this exhilarating journey of turning your ideas into tangible, impactful ventures.

Creativity lies at the heart of every successful entrepreneur as a potent force. It is like fuel; it ignites the spark of innovation, propelling individuals to challenge the status quo, reimagine possibilities, and drive meaningful change. Creativity, in its myriad forms, has the power to disrupt industries, solve complex problems, and create solutions that have a lasting impact on the lives of individuals and the broader society.

Throughout these pages, we will look at how important creativity is in entrepreneurship. We'll look at how developing your creative potential can lead you on a transforming journey to success. But it is not just about the individual pursuit of success; it is about making a difference, leaving a lasting imprint, and creating a positive impact that resonates far beyond the confines of your entrepreneurial journey.

As you embark on this journey of self-discovery and entrepreneurial exploration, keep in mind that you have an abundance of creativity inside you just waiting to be released.
This book will serve as your guiding light, illuminating the path

and providing inspiration, knowledge, and actionable insights to help you navigate the terrain of entrepreneurship and ignite your creative potential.

Now, let us set forth on this exhilarating adventure, where ideas take shape, impact is born, and the entrepreneurial spirit soars. Together, we will journey from idea to impact, shaping a future defined by the transformative power of your creative endeavors.

PART ONE

Discover Your Entrepreneurial Path

CHAPTER 1: SETTING THE STAGE

The world brims with opportunities and challenges; if you have a vision, a drive, and a hunger for innovation, the journey of entrepreneurship beckons you. In entrepreneurship, the ordinary can be transformed into the extraordinary and dreams sculpted into reality. This voyage isn't merely about creating a product or service; it's about shaping the future, disrupting the status quo, and leaving an indelible mark on the canvas of human progress.

Every successful entrepreneurial story begins with a spark—an idea, a concept, or a passion that refuses to remain dormant. This spark ignites the flames of possibility within, propelling them to venture beyond their comfort zones and explore uncharted territories. It's a call to action, an invitation to contribute, and a challenge to create something that resonates with the world.

The Entrepreneurial Mindset

At the heart of every transformative entrepreneurial journey lies the entrepreneurial mindset—a unique way of thinking that merges creativity, resilience, and a willingness to learn. Entrepreneurs see problems as opportunities in disguise, uncovering solutions where others see roadblocks.

This way of thinking is unrestricted by conventional wisdom. It embraces failure not as a defeat but as a lesson—a stepping stone to success. The fierce determination to iterate, adapt, and evolve, relentlessly pushing the limits of what is possible, is a hallmark of the entrepreneurial spirit.

The lifeblood of the entrepreneurial mindset is innovation. It's about looking at the world from a different perspective, identifying gaps that need filling and coming up with solutions that make a difference.

So, as we embark on this journey together, let's cast aside the familiar and be willing to embrace the unknown. Let's explore the entrepreneur world, where imagination knows no bounds. Passion is the compass; the entrepreneurial mindset paves the way for building the tomorrow you want to be proud of. The stage is set, and the curtain rises on a narrative of innovation, resilience, and the unwavering pursuit of a brighter tomorrow.

The Power of Passion

"Passion is the fuel that drives entrepreneurs to push boundaries, overcome challenges, and create something extraordinary." - Richard Branson

Entrepreneurship is more than starting a business; it's about following your dreams, pursuing your interests, and finding innovative ways to solve problems. It requires a deep connection with your inner self, a burning desire to make a difference, and the will to persevere through triumphs and setbacks.

In her book "Grit: The Power of Passion and Perseverance," psychologist Angela Duckworth highlights the significance of passion in achieving long-term goals. She emphasizes that those who are deeply passionate about their pursuits are more likely to persist in the face of challenges and setbacks, increasing their chances of entrepreneurial success.

Passion is a driving force; it propels beyond the boundaries of the ordinary into the realm of extraordinary accomplishment. It's like a spark; it ignites the flames of innovation, fuels determination, and turns dreams into reality. In entrepreneurship, passion is the foundation of a successful venture.

It is the force that propels you forward, even in the face of adversity; it fuels your unwavering dedication to your vision. Passion is the transformative power you need to make a significant impact.

Steve Jobs, the co-founder of Apple Inc., once said, "People with passion can change the world." Passion fuels determination, perseverance, and the ability to overcome obstacles, making it a crucial ingredient for entrepreneurial success.

In his seminal work, "The Lean Startup: How Today's Entrepreneurs Use Continuous Innovation to Create Radically Successful Businesses," Eric Ries emphasizes the pivotal role of passion in the entrepreneurial journey. Ries, an entrepreneur and author, offers insightful advice on the mindset needed to find and nurture one's drive for entrepreneurship.
Ries contends that true entrepreneurial passion stems from a deep connection to a problem or opportunity in the world. It is an intrinsic desire to make a meaningful difference and address a pressing need.

As he puts it, "Entrepreneurs are driven by an intense desire to change the world, to solve a problem that deeply bothers them or to seize a fleeting opportunity. They cannot help but be passionate about what they do; it is an integral part of who they are."

"Your work is going to fill a large part of your life, and the only way to be truly satisfied is to do what you believe is great work. And the only way to do great work is to love what you do." - Steve Jobs.

Steve Jobs emphasized the importance of loving what you do. When you have a genuine passion for your work, it ceases to feel like a chore and becomes an integral part of who you are. Find something that resonates with your core values, aligns with your strengths, and allows you to make a positive impact. Your entrepreneurial journey should be driven by a deep sense of purpose and the desire to create something great.

Passion and creativity go hand in hand. When you have a genuine passion for what you do, you are more willing to take risks and think outside the box. Entrepreneurship is inherently about innovation, and being willing to step outside your comfort zone is essential for discovering new opportunities and finding unique solutions.

"The only limit to our realization of tomorrow will be our doubts of today." - Franklin D. Roosevelt.

It's natural to have doubts and fears along your entrepreneurial journey. However, it's crucial to remember that doubt is the enemy of progress. Embrace the uncertainty and use it as fuel to propel yourself forward. Have faith in your abilities, trust the process, and don't let self-doubt hinder your pursuit of passion.

"Passion is the oxygen of the soul." - Billie Jean King.

Passion breathes life into your entrepreneurial journey, infusing every action with purpose and vitality. Billie Jean King perfectly put it as the "oxygen of the soul." Cultivate your passion, nurture it, and let it guide you through the ups and downs of entrepreneurship.

"Success is not the key to happiness. Happiness is the key to success. If you love what you are doing, you will be successful." - Albert Schweitzer.

Albert Schweitzer reminds us that true success lies in finding happiness in what we do. As you explore your entrepreneurial passion, prioritize your own happiness and well-being. Success will come if you create a business that makes you happy and fulfilled.

"Your time is limited, so don't waste it living someone else's life. Don't be trapped by dogma, which is living with the results of other people's thinking." - Steve Jobs

In the pursuit of your entrepreneurial passion, it's essential to forge your own path and resist the temptation to conform to societal expectations. Avoid getting trapped in other people's ideas of success or adhering to conventional wisdom. Instead, trust your instincts, think independently, and embrace your unique vision. Your passion is what sets you apart; let it guide your decisions and lead you to extraordinary places.

"Passion is contagious; if you're passionate about something, others will be too." - Susan Cain.

Passion is both a personal motivator and a catalyst for inspiring others. When you are truly passionate about what you do, your enthusiasm spreads. It attracts like-minded individuals, customers, and collaborators who share your vision and amplify your impact.

"Passion is the genesis of genius." - Tony Robbins.

Passion has the remarkable ability to unlock your potential and ignite your inner genius.

Believe in the beauty of your entrepreneurial dreams, and let your passion guide you towards a future that exceeds your wildest imagination. The world awaits your unique contribution. Embrace your entrepreneurial spirit, and let it soar.

Ignite Your Entrepreneurial Spirit

"The best way to predict the future is to create it." - Peter Drucker

Starting a successful entrepreneurial journey requires discovering and nurturing your entrepreneurial passion. Understanding what truly drives and motivates you can provide a solid foundation for your business ventures.

In this chapter, we will explore the key steps to help you uncover your entrepreneurial passion, drawing insights from renowned authors and experts in the field.

As you embark on this path, it's important to remember that passion cannot be forced or manufactured; it is a genuine and authentic expression of who you are and what you love. While some people may discover their passion effortlessly, others might need a spark to ignite their entrepreneurial spirit. Here are a few ideas to help you reawaken and sustain what drives you.

- **Reflect on Your Interests and Talents.** Begin your entrepreneurial journey with introspection. Take time to think deeply about your interests and abilities. Consider the areas of life that truly resonate with you. What activities light up your soul? What makes you come alive? These are the foundations of your entrepreneurial passion.

As entrepreneur and author Steve Blank noted, begin with understanding your motivations, skills, and passion. Look back on your life experiences, hobbies, and personal interests. In these moments, you'll find the seeds of your entrepreneurial potential.

- **Identify Your Values.** Your core values are the compass guiding your entrepreneurial journey. They define who you are and how you want to live.

Take time to reflect on what matters most to you in life and business. What principles do you want to embody as an entrepreneur? You will discover a deeper sense of purpose and fulfillment by aligning your passion with your values.

- **Set Meaningful Goals.** Passion is fueled by purpose. Set objectives that are in line with your passion. Having a sense of purpose can enhance your commitment and drive. Each milestone you achieve brings you closer to your ultimate vision.

- **Seek Inspiration and Role Models.** Surround yourself with kindred spirits who share your passions. Engage in discussions and collaborations with others who are enthusiastic about similar areas. This interaction may assist you in clarifying your own passion.

Jim Rohn wisely said, "You are the average of the five people you spend the most time with." Reid Hoffman, the co-founder of LinkedIn, advised, "The fastest way to change yourself is to hang out with people who are already the way you want to be."

- **Explore Diverse Industries and Sectors.** Investigate various industries and sectors to broaden your perspective and find potential areas of interest.

Eric Ries emphasized the importance of this exploration, stating, "Expose yourself to as many ideas and fields as possible. This will help you discover new interests and find areas that align with your passion."

- **Identify Problems and Opportunities.** Entrepreneurial passion often ignites when you identify problems or untapped opportunities in the market.

Nobel laureate Muhammad Yunus stated, "Entrepreneurs should continuously be on the lookout for unmet needs and social problems that can be solved through innovative solutions." Pay attention to the challenges confronting people and think critically about how you can contribute with unique solutions. This problem-solving process can lead to the discovery of your true entrepreneurial calling.

- **Continuous Learning.** In your chosen field, immerse yourself in learning. The more you know, the more likely you'll uncover aspects that fuel your passion and present new avenues for exploration. Embrace the uncertainty and challenges that come with entrepreneurship.

Guy Kawasaki wisely wrote in "The Art of the Start 2.0." These challenges will test your dedication and resilience, and your passion will act as a driving force during difficult times. Richard Branson advises, "Entrepreneurship is not about getting rich quick; it's about creating something new and making a positive difference."

CHAPTER 2: NAVIGATING ENTREPRENEURIAL CHALLENGES AND OVERCOMING OBSTACLES

The entrepreneurial journey is like a maze filled with unexpected twists and turns. Its path is strewn with challenges, but they are opportunities in disguise.

In this chapter, we'll explore how you, as an aspiring entrepreneur, can approach challenges with a proactive mindset and employ effective strategies to overcome them.

The entrepreneurial journey is not without its fair share of challenges and obstacles. Entrepreneurs come across different kinds of challenges that can impede their progress. These tests separate the determined from the disheartened and the resilient from the defeated.

Understanding these challenges will equip you with crucial skills for devising effective solutions. This section explores the common challenges faced by entrepreneurs and provides strategies for overcoming them to ensure your venture's long-term success.

Common Challenges Faced By Entrepreneurs

- **Financial Constraints.** Limited access to capital and funding can hinder business growth and development. You need to explore funding options, manage finances wisely, and seek investors or loans.

- **Market Competition.** Competing with established players and new entrants is a significant challenge. You can stay competitive by differentiating your offerings, identifying unique selling points, and focusing on delivering superior value to customers.

- **Uncertain Market Demand.** Predicting market demand accurately, especially for innovative products or services, can be tough and challenging. Conduct thorough market research, gather customer feedback, and iterate your offerings based on market needs.

- **Regulatory Compliance.** Navigating complex and evolving regulations is a critical challenge for entrepreneurs. To ensure compliance and mitigate legal risks, keep abreast on legal standards and seek professional guidance.

- **Team Building and Management.** Bringing together a skilled and motivated team is crucial for every entrepreneurial venture. Building a successful enterprise requires hiring talented individuals, fostering a positive work culture, providing effective leadership, and addressing team dynamics.

Embrace Challenges as Opportunities

Richard Branson, an author and entrepreneur, once stated, "The brave may not live forever, but the cautious do not live at all."

This sentiment summarizes the principle of entrepreneurship - the willingness to take calculated risks in pursuit of opportunities. Successful entrepreneurs understand that taking risks is an integral part of the journey. They assess the potential rewards, weigh the risks, and make informed decisions. Embracing risk requires a balance of courage and calculated decision-making.

Research by Saras Sarasvathy, author of "Effectuation: Elements of Entrepreneurial Expertise," suggests that successful entrepreneurs take a strategic approach, focusing on what they can control and leveraging their available resources.

Embrace the idea, as suggested by Carol Dweck, that your abilities and intelligence can evolve with effort and learning. Challenges become chances to expand your skill set and broaden your horizons.

Strategies for Overcoming Obstacles

As you embark on your entrepreneurial journey, it's essential to employ various strategies to deal with problems effectively. Just as Steve Jobs emphasized meticulous planning, it's crucial to anticipate potential challenges and develop contingency plans. As Jobs noted, perseverance often stands as the distinguishing factor between success and failure. Let's see some strategies that will help you tackle challenges.

- **Strategic Planning and Risk Management.** Begin with a comprehensive business plan and thorough risk assessments. These preparations enable you to anticipate challenges and formulate strategies to mitigate them. A well-defined roadmap and contingency plans significantly enhance your ability to overcome obstacles.

View challenges as catalysts for innovation, much like great entrepreneurs such as Elon Musk. Embrace formidable obstacles as opportunities to refine your products or services, making them better, more efficient, and more marketable.

- **Financial Management.** Effective financial management is fundamental for the survival and growth of your venture. To ensure financial stability, maintain precise financial records, closely monitor cash flow, exercise cost control, and explore diverse funding options.

- **Learn from Failures.** Failure is an inevitable part of the entrepreneurial journey. Don't see it as insurmountable roadblocks, but as valuable opportunities for growth and learning.

Zig Ziglar wisely stated, "Failure is an event, not a person." This perspective underscores the importance of separating failures from personal identity and using them as stepping stones to success. Developing a problem-solving mindset is essential to handling failures.

Psychologist Carol Dweck's research highlights the significance of a growth mindset in approaching challenges and embracing failure as a catalyst for growth.

- **Foster Creative Problem-Solving.** Overcoming entrepreneurial challenges demands creative problem-solving ability. Utilize your creative thinking skills to devise innovative solutions to complex problems.

If you foster a culture of creative problem-solving within your team, your business will thrive. Create an environment where unique ideas are valued and encouraged.

- **Continuous Innovation and Differentiation.** Foster a culture of creativity, embrace technological advancements, and strive to offer unique value propositions that set your business apart.

- **Seek Inspiration from Others.** You will find motivation and guidance from the stories of others who overcame significant challenges to achieve success.

CHAPTER 3: GENERATING IMPACTFUL IDEAS

The ability to generate impactful ideas is your compass; it steers you toward success. Your innovative ideas form the core of your venture, setting it apart in a crowded marketplace.

This chapter will guide you through the creative process of idea generation, the crucial steps of refining and evaluating those ideas, and finally, the transformative process of turning your ideas into actionable plans.

By the end of this chapter, you'll be equipped with the knowledge and skills to breathe life into your entrepreneurial dreams.

Creative Process of Idea Generation

Idea generation marks the inception of your entrepreneurial journey. It involves recognizing opportunities in your environment, pinpointing existing problems, and conceiving innovative solutions. To embark on this imaginative process, follow these steps.

- **Observation.** Commence by closely observing your surroundings and industry. Pay attention to emerging trends, consumer behavior, and the evolution of technology.

Remember Steve Jobs' insight: "You can't connect the dots looking forward; you can only connect them looking backwards."

- **Brainstorming Ideas.** Foster brainstorming sessions involving diverse teams. Different perspectives frequently yield unique insights. Keep in mind, during brainstorming, no idea is unworthy – they possess the potential to flourish.

- **Research and Market Analysis.** Validate your concepts through comprehensive research. Determine if there's demand for your idea. Assess your competition and ascertain what sets your business apart. Utilize tools like surveys, interviews, and market research to gather data.

- **Identify Customer Needs.** Take the time to empathize with your target customers. Understand their needs and challenges. This empathetic approach allows you to identify opportunities for creating products or services that genuinely cater to their requirements.

- **Unique Selling Proposition (USP).** Deliberate on what distinguishes your business idea from others in the market. Identify your unique selling proposition (USP) – that special feature or benefit that sets your idea apart. This will enable you to differentiate yourself and attract customers.

- **Continuous Improvement and Validation.** Embrace an iterative approach to idea development. Embrace feedback and be prepared to make alterations and enhancements along the way. The process of refinement and iteration is pivotal for transforming a good idea into a great one and validating its potential in the real market.

- **Self-Belief.** Have faith in yourself and your ideas. Trust your instincts and have confidence in your abilities. Entrepreneurship necessitates perseverance and faith in your capacity to make an impact. Stay motivated and resilient as you actualize your impactful business idea.

Refining and Evaluating Ideas

Once you've generated a pool of ideas, it's time to separate the diamonds from the rough. Refining and evaluating your idea is essential to ensure that your resources are allocated to workable concepts.

- **Feasibility.** Assess the feasibility of each idea. Do you have the resources, skills, and technology required to bring this idea to life? Focus on ideas with a realistic chance of success and scalability.

- **Prototyping and Testing.** Construct prototypes or minimum viable products (MVPs) to assess your ideas. These prototypes can be rudimentary versions of your product or service designed to gather feedback from potential customers. Use their suggestions to improve and refine your concept.

- **Scalability**. Consider whether the idea can grow into a sustainable business. Scalability is essential for long-term success.

- **Risk Assessment.** Consider the dangers and difficulties that each idea might present. How will you mitigate these risks?

Transforming Ideas into Actionable Plans

After you've refined your ideas, the next step is to put them into actionable plans that will drive your entrepreneurial journey forward.

- **Goal Setting.** Clearly define your goals and objectives. What do you want to achieve with this idea? Having specific goals will keep you focused and motivated.

- **Resource Allocation.** Determine the resources required to implement your idea, including finances, manpower, and technology.

- **Timeline.** Create a timeline or project plan. Break down the implementation process into manageable milestones with deadlines.

- **Risk Management.** Develop strategies to mitigate risks and handle potential obstacles that may arise during implementation.

- **Continuous Learning.** Embrace a culture of continuous learning and adaptation. As you execute your plans, be open to feedback and be willing to pivot if necessary.

Idea generation is the heartbeat of entrepreneurship. Remember, every great business started with a single idea. It's your dedication, persistence, and ability to innovate that will determine your success. As Thomas Edison said, "Genius is 1% inspiration and 99% perspiration."

So, let your ideas flow and be prepared to work tirelessly to bring them to life. Your entrepreneurial journey awaits, filled with the promise of impact and innovation.

Part 2

Understanding Your Market and Customers

CHAPTER 4: USING EMPATHY TO UNDERSTAND CUSTOMER NEEDS AND CREATE VALUE

Understanding your customers is not just a skill; it is an art. Your ability to empathize with them can spell the difference between a thriving business and one that fades into obscurity.

This chapter will delve into the essence of empathy in entrepreneurship, equipping you with techniques for deep customer understanding and guiding you in creating solutions that are not just customer-centric but profoundly aligned with their needs and desires.

The Essence of Empathy in Entrepreneurship

Empathy is an incredible superpower when it comes to entrepreneurship. It could completely alter how you conduct business and how you relate to your customers. Empathy is not just a buzzword; it's an essential ingredient for success.

Empathy, regarded as the foundation of entrepreneurship, is the ability to truly grasp and feel the emotions, thoughts, and your customers' experiences. It goes beyond surface-level interactions and delves into the core of human connection.

Empathy isn't a fleeting emotion; it's a continuous practice that informs your decisions and actions. In the words of Steve Jobs, "You've got to start with the customer experience and work backwards to the technology."

When you put yourself in your customers' shoes, something magical happens. You gain a deep understanding of their needs, desires, and pain points. You start to see the world through their eyes, and that perspective is pure gold. It allows you to develop products and services that truly resonate with them, solve their problems, and better their lives.

But empathy doesn't stop at understanding. It goes beyond that. It's about genuinely caring for your customers and their well-being. When you empathize with them, you build a connection, a bond based on trust and authenticity. You become more than just a business; you become a partner, and you genuinely want to help make a difference.

This connection is what sets you apart from the competition. In a world filled with impersonal transactions and faceless corporations, empathy humanizes your business. It creates a customer experience that is memorable, meaningful, and delightful. People want to do business with those who understand them, listen to them, and genuinely care.

But the power of empathy doesn't stop with your customers. It extends to your team as well. When you empathize with your employees, you create a positive and supportive work environment. You understand their strengths, weaknesses, and aspirations. You become a leader who inspires and motivates, someone who fosters collaboration and growth.

Empathy also helps you navigate the ups and downs of entrepreneurship. It allows you to handle challenges with grace and resilience. By putting yourself in the shoes of your customers and your team, you can anticipate their needs, address their concerns, and find innovative solutions. Empathy becomes your compass, guiding you through the ever-changing landscape of business.

So, learn to listen, understand, and genuinely care. You can create a business that makes a real difference in people's lives.

Techniques for Deep Customer Understanding

You can use a variety of strategies to connect with and understand your customers on a deeper level.

- **Active Listening.** When interacting with customers, practice active listening. Pay close attention to their words, tone, and body language. Strive to comprehend their underlying feelings and concerns.

- **Put Yourself in Their Shoes.** Imagine yourself in the customer's position, facing the challenges or frustrations they might be experiencing. Through this exercise, you can better comprehend their viewpoint and approach the situation with empathy and compassion.

- **Surveys and Feedback Loops.** Utilize surveys, feedback forms, and suggestion boxes to gather insights directly from your customers. These tools provide structured ways to collect valuable information.

- **Ask Open-Ended Questions.** Encourage customers to share their thoughts and feelings by asking open-ended questions. This not only provides useful information but also shows that you genuinely care about their experiences and opinions.

- **Reflect and Validate Their Emotions.** When customers express their frustrations or concerns, reflect their emotions to them to show that you understand and empathize with their feelings. You create a safe space for them to open up and trust that their concerns are being heard and taken seriously by acknowledging their emotions.

- **Seek to Understand Their Goals**. Take the time to understand the specific goals and desires of each customer. This will help you align your solutions with their needs and aspirations. Understanding what they hope to achieve equips you to tailor your approach to provide meaningful value and support their journey.

- **Practice Patience and Empathy.** Approach customers with patience and empathy when they are upset or frustrated. Remind yourself that their emotions are legitimate, and your role is to assist and support them, even in difficult situations. Staying calm and empathic can aid in the de-escalation of tense situations and the discovery of effective solutions.

- **Continuously Learn and Improve.** Actively seek out customer feedback and take the chance to learn and grow from it. Appreciate their insights and take them to heart, as they help you better understand their needs and provide a better experience moving forward.

- **Observational Research.** Sometimes, what customers do speaks louder than what they say. Observe their behaviors, preferences, and pain points by analyzing their interactions with your product or service.

- **User Personas.** Create detailed user personas representing your ideal customers. These personas should include demographic information, goals, challenges, and motivations. Personas serve as reference points for decision-making.

- **Empathy Mapping.** Develop empathy maps, which are visual representations of what your customers are thinking, feeling, seeing, saying, and doing. It will assist you in comprehending their inner world.

- **Customer Journey Mapping.** Plot the entire customer journey, from awareness to post-purchase, to identify touch points, pain points, and opportunities for improvement. Providing a comprehensive view will help you to gain a better understanding of the customer experience and to make informed improvements.

It's important to have empathy, not just as a skill but also as a mindset that helps you build meaningful relationships based on trust, understanding, and mutual respect rather than just completing transactions.

Creating Solutions Aligned with Customer Needs

Empathy isn't merely about understanding; it's about taking action. Once you've gathered insights into your customers' world, it's time to create solutions that resonate with their needs and desires.

- **Iterative Design.** To guarantee alignment with your customers evolving needs, use an iterative design approach to consistently enhance your product or service in response to their feedback.

- **Co-Creation.** Involve customers in your design process. Co-creation sessions or focus groups can yield innovative ideas and validate existing ones.

- **Prototype and Test.** To reduce the possibility of creating something that does not meet customer expectations. Create samples or minimum viable products (MVPs) to test your ideas with real people. Throughout the prototyping process, remain laser-focused on delivering value to your customers. Constantly ask yourself:

➢ "How does this solution solve their problem?"

➢ "How does it improve their experience?"

This customer-centric mindset will drive you to go beyond surface-level features and dive deeper into creating solutions that have a lasting impact.

- **Feedback Loops.** Establish feedback loops to capture ongoing input from customers. Make them feel heard, valued, and part of the solution.

- **Embrace Failure.** Understand that not every idea will succeed. Failure is an opportunity to learn and adapt. Embrace it as a stepping stone towards creating better solutions.

Empathy is a game-changer when it comes to designing customer-centric solutions. It allows us to truly understand our customers' needs, desires, and challenges and helps us create meaningful and valuable experiences for them. Understand that not every idea will succeed. Failure is an opportunity to learn and adapt. Embrace it as a stepping stone towards creating better solutions.

CHAPTER 5: CRAFTING YOUR BUSINESS MODEL

When embarking on an entrepreneurial journey, one of the fundamental aspects that can make or break your venture is crafting a robust business model. A well-designed business model is akin to architecting the foundation of a grand skyscraper. It is the backbone of your business and guides you to long-term success. It's the structural design upon which your entire entrepreneurial venture rests.

In this chapter, we'll demystify the intricacies of a business model, explore the essential elements of a robust model, and discover how to design a model that paves your path to success.

Demystifying the Business Model

"A business model," as esteemed professor and author Alexander Osterwalder explains, "is the rationale of how an organization creates, delivers, and captures value."
In simpler terms, it's the blueprint that outlines how your business operates, generates revenue, and ultimately thrives.

- **Value Proposition.** The core of your business model starts with understanding the needs and desires of your target audience.

- **What unique value are you offering?** Your value

proposition should clearly articulate what sets your product or service apart from the competition.

- **Customer Segments.** Every business caters to a specific set of customers. Define your target audience - their demographics, preferences, and pain points. Tailor your offerings to address their needs effectively.

- **Channels.** Consider how you will reach your customers. Will it be through a physical store, an e-commerce website, or a combination of the two? Your distribution channels must correspond to the preferences of your target audience.

- **Revenue Streams.** How will your business make money? Identify various revenue streams, such as direct sales, subscriptions, or advertising. Ensure they align with your value proposition and customer segments.

Elements of a Robust Business Model

A robust business model comprises various interconnected elements that work together to create a sustainable and profitable venture. Here are essential components to consider.

- **Clear Revenue Streams.** Diversify your income sources. Whether it's through product sales, subscriptions, licensing, or other means, having multiple revenue streams can enhance your financial stability.

- **Customer Relationships.** Cultivating strong customer relationships is vital. Consider whether you will provide exceptional customer service, online support, or a self-service model—choose an approach that resonates with your customer segments.

- **Customer-Centric Value.** Your business model should center on providing exceptional value to your customers. This value should be meaningful and distinct from what competitors offer.

- **Efficient Cost Management.** Keep a close eye on your cost structure. Efficient resource allocation and cost management are vital for maintaining profitability.

- **Flexibility and Adaptability.** The business landscape is ever-evolving. Your model should be flexible enough to adapt to changing market conditions and customer demands.

- **Key Activities.** Identify the day-to-day operations that make your business function smoothly. Whether it's product development, marketing, or distribution, these activities are critical to your success.

- **Key Partnerships.** Collaborations with other businesses can be game-changers. Partnerships can help you access resources or customers that would be challenging to reach alone.

- **Key Resources.** Identify the resources you need to deliver your value proposition. Resources can be in the form of tangible goods like machinery, intangible assets like intellectual property, or human resources like talented workers.

- **Scalability.** Scalability is a vital component of an effective business model. As your business expands, your costs shouldn't grow at the same rate, allowing for increased profitability.

Designing Your Business Model for Success

Designing a business model for success involves a combination of creativity and pragmatism. Here's a step-by-step guide.

- **Market Research.** Begin by thoroughly researching your target market. Understanding your customers' needs, preferences, and pain points forms the foundation of your value proposition.

- **Stay Customer-Centric.** Keep an eye on the changing needs of your customers and make necessary model adjustments. Failure is a given for any business model that doesn't reflect the needs of the target market.

- **Channels and Distribution.** Choose the most suitable channels to reach your customers. This might include online platforms, physical stores, or a combination of both.

- **Keep an Eye on the Competition.** Study your competitors' business models. What are they doing well, and where are they falling short? Learn from their successes and mistakes.

- **Adapt to Market Dynamics.** Markets change. New technologies emerge. Be ready to pivot if necessary. For example, Netflix started as a DVD rental service and transformed into a streaming giant.

- **Value Proposition.** Create a compelling value proposition that addresses a specific customer problem or need. Your solution should stand out in the market.

- **Revenue Model.** Determine your pricing strategy. Consider factors like production costs, competition, and perceived value to set competitive prices.

- **Resource Allocation.** Allocate your resources wisely. Focus on what's critical to delivering your value proposition and achieving your business goals.

- **Testing and Iteration.** Your initial business model might not be perfect. Be ready to iterate and adapt as you gather real-world feedback and data.

- **Long-Term Sustainability.** Plan for growth and expansion by ensuring that your business model is not only profitable in the short term but also sustainable over the long haul.

Part 3
Establishing a Strong Foundation

CHAPTER 6: BUILDING A SOLID FOUNDATION

As you continue down this path, one of the critical steps in ensuring your venture's long-term success is laying a solid foundation. In this chapter, we'll explore two vital aspects of building this foundation: Legal and Organizational Considerations and Structuring Your Business for Growth.

Legal and Organizational Considerations

Before you enter into your entrepreneurial pursuits, you must first understand the complex legal structure that controls businesses. Taking the time to address these concerns early on will help you avoid potential issues later on.

- **Business Structure.** The first decision you'll need to make is the legal structure of your business. Common business structures include sole proprietorships, partnerships; limited liability companies (LLCs), corporations, and others. Each has advantages and downsides; pick the option that matches your objectives and level of risk tolerance.

- **Registration and Licensing.** Depending on your location and business type, you might need to register your business with the appropriate government authorities and obtain licenses and permits. These requirements vary widely, so be sure to research your specific obligations.

- **Intellectual Property Protection.** If your business relies on unique ideas, products, or services, safeguarding your intellectual property is paramount. Consider trademarks, copyrights, and patents to protect your innovations.

- **Taxation.** Understanding your tax obligations is essential. Consult a tax specialist to ensure that you comply with all local, state, and federal tax regulations.

- **Contracts and Agreements.** Contracts with partners, employees, suppliers, or customers must be unambiguous and legally binding. These documents set expectations, protect your interests, and give redress in the event of a dispute.

Structuring Your Business for Growth

Now that the legal foundation is established, it's time to focus on creating an organizational structure that will support your company's growth aspirations.

- **Business Plan.** Start with a comprehensive business plan that outlines your vision, mission, goals, and strategies. This document will serve as a roadmap for your journey, helping you stay on course and secure financing if needed.

- **Financing Options.** Depending on your business's nature and needs, explore financing options like loans, grants, angel investors, venture capital, or crowdfunding. Carefully evaluate each to determine the best fit.

- **Team Building.** No successful business is built alone. As your venture grows, consider assembling a team with complementary skills and a shared passion for your mission. Hiring and retaining top talent will be instrumental in your success.

- **Technology and Infrastructure.** Invest in the right technology and infrastructure to support your operations efficiently. Embrace digital tools for tasks like accounting, marketing, and communication to streamline processes.

- **Scalability Planning.** Scalability is the ability of your business to handle growth efficiently. Consider how your operations, technology, and workforce will adapt as your customer base expands. By putting a scaling plan in place, your company can avoid bottlenecks and take advantage of opportunities as they present themselves.

- **Risk Management.** Anticipate and mitigate potential risks to your business, such as market fluctuations, supply chain disruptions, or cybersecurity threats. A robust risk management strategy can protect your investments.

Building a solid foundation for your business is not a one-time task but an ongoing commitment. Continually assess and adapt your legal and organizational structures to ensure they align with your evolving goals and market conditions.

In the next chapter, we'll delve into the exciting world of marketing and branding, helping you create a strong presence in your chosen market.

CHAPTER 7: MARKETING AND BRANDING FOR IMPACT

Making an emotional connection with your audience is a key component of marketing, which goes beyond simply promoting your goods or services. Consider it as a conversation with potential customers.

Famous marketing expert Philip Kotler once said: "Marketing is not the art of finding clever ways to dispose of what you make. It is the art of creating genuine customer value."

This chapter will guide you through the art of effective marketing, developing your brand identity, and reaching your target audience, providing you with the tools to make a significant impact.

The Art of Effective Marketing

Effective marketing begins with understanding your customers deeply. Effective marketing is the cornerstone of successful entrepreneurship. It's not just about promoting your product or service; it's about crafting a compelling narrative that resonates with your audience. Here are some key principles to consider.

- **Know Your Audience.** To effectively market your offering, you must first understand your target audience. Conduct market research to identify their needs, preferences, and pain points. Develop detailed buyer personas that represent your ideal customers. This will help you tailor your marketing efforts to their specific needs and preferences.

- **Invest in a strong online presence.** In today's digital age, your website and social media profiles are often the first touch points customers have with your brand. Choose the platforms that align with your audience's demographics and preferences, and consistently engage with your followers.

- **Create Compelling Content.** Content is king in the digital age. Leverage content marketing, such as blog posts, videos, and infographics, to provide value and build trust with your audience. Develop high-quality, valuable content that educates, entertains, or solves problems for your audience.

- **Optimize for SEO.** Search engine optimization (SEO) is vital for online visibility. Ensure your website and content are optimized for relevant keywords to improve your ranking in search engine results.

- **Measure and Adjust.** Use analytics tools to track the performance of your marketing efforts. Monitor key metrics like website traffic, conversion rates, and social media engagement. Adjust your strategies based on the data.

Developing Your Brand Identity

Your brand is more than simply a logo; it is the perception that people have of your company. Building a strong brand identity is critical for establishing trust and recognition. Here's how to accomplish it.

- **Define Your Brand.** Start by clearly defining your brand's mission, values, and unique selling proposition (USP). What sets your business apart from the competition? Your USP should be at the heart of your brand identity.

- **Create a Memorable Logo.** Your logo is a visual representation of your brand. It should be simple, memorable, and reflect your brand's personality. Consider hiring a professional designer for this crucial task.

- **Craft Your Brand Story.** Storytelling is a powerful tool for building an emotional connection with your audience. Share the story of why you started your business and how it can make a difference in people's lives.

- **Consistency is Key.** Ensure that your brand elements, such as colors, fonts, and tone of voice, remain consistent across all touch points, from your website to your social media profiles.

- **Build Trust.** Trust is the foundation of a strong brand. Deliver your promises, provide excellent customer service, and actively engage with your audience to build trust over time.

CHAPTER 8: LEADING WITH PURPOSE AND CREATING LASTING CHANGE

As our entrepreneurial journey in this book nears the end, remember that leading with purpose is the compass that will direct you to make a lasting impact. Navigating the complex corporate world as a leader transcends the traditional conceptions of authority and management. It's about being a change agent, a leader who motivates their team as well as the entire entrepreneurial ecosystem.

The Essence of Purpose-Driven Leadership

Purpose-driven leadership is the cornerstone of your entrepreneurial legacy. At its core, it's about aligning your business endeavors with a deeper mission and a set of values that are beyond profit margins. It's the belief that your work should leave the world a better place.

Why Purpose Matters?

Purpose infuses meaning into your actions. It galvanizes your team and stakeholders. Research by McKinsey & Company indicates that companies with a clear sense of purpose are more likely to outperform their peers. It drives innovation, enhances employee engagement, and fosters customer loyalty.

Your purpose as an entrepreneur might be to solve a pressing societal problem, empower underserved communities, or revolutionize an industry with groundbreaking technology. Regardless of its nature, your purpose becomes the guiding star that shapes your business decisions, informs your strategies, and influences your company culture.

Nurturing a Culture of Impact and Innovation

Creating lasting change requires an environment where innovation flourishes and impact is celebrated. Your role as a leader is to cultivate this culture within your organization. Encourage your team to think creatively and embrace experimentation.

Google's "20% Time" policy, which allows employees to dedicate a portion of their workweek to pursuing personal projects, is a prime example. It has led to the development of groundbreaking products like Gmail and Google Maps.

Furthermore, collaboration is key. Promote cross-functional teamwork and diversity of thought. Research by Deloitte demonstrates that diverse teams are more innovative and have a greater potential for financial success.

Leaving a Legacy through Entrepreneurship

Entrepreneurial journey is not just about the present; it's about the legacy you leave for future generations. It's about creating a business that stands the test of time, making a difference, and inspiring others to follow suit.

Integrate sustainability into your business practices. Reduce your carbon footprint, minimize waste, and support ethical supply chains. Patagonia, a company known for its commitment to sustainability, is an exemplar in this regard.

Engage in social responsibility. Give back to the community through initiatives like corporate social responsibility programs. TOMS, renowned for its "One for One" model, exemplifies how businesses can create lasting change.

Leading with purpose in entrepreneurship is not only about financial success but also about making a meaningful impact. It's about fostering a culture of innovation and leaving a legacy that inspires others to embark on their own purpose-driven journeys.

Your leadership has the potential to change not only your life but also the world. Embrace it with passion, dedication, and a commitment to a higher purpose, and you will truly create lasting change.

CONCLUSION AND NEXT STEPS

As you conclude this entrepreneurial journey, take a moment to pause and reflect on the incredible path you've traversed. Your quest began with a spark of passion and curiosity, and it has led you through the labyrinthine corridors of innovation, challenges, and boundless opportunities.

You've ventured into uncharted territory, learned invaluable lessons, and honed your skills. Now, it's time to absorb the wisdom gained and prepare for the ever-evolving nature of entrepreneurship.

Embrace the Continual Learning Journey

Entrepreneurship is not a destination; it's a dynamic, ever-changing voyage. The business landscape constantly shifts, driven by technological advancements, economic fluctuations, and shifting consumer behaviors.

To thrive, you must be a perpetual learner. Stay curious, stay hungry for knowledge. Seek out emerging trends, attend workshops, and connect with mentors who can guide you through uncharted waters.

Resilience in the Face of Adversity

Throughout your journey, you've encountered obstacles and setbacks. Remember that resilience is your greatest asset.

Entrepreneurship is not about avoiding failure but about learning from it. The most successful entrepreneurs have faced adversity head-on, using it as a stepping stone to higher achievements. Let each challenge you've overcome fuel your determination to persevere.

Adaptability: Your Secret Weapon

The ability to adapt is paramount. Be prepared to pivot when necessary, adjusting your strategies and approaches as circumstances change. What worked yesterday may not work tomorrow, and flexibility can be the key to survival. Continually assess your business model and be willing to make calculated changes to stay relevant.

Building a Legacy

Entrepreneurship is not just about personal success; it's about leaving a lasting impact on your community, industry, or the world. Consider how your work contributes to the greater good. Are you solving real problems?

Are you making the world a better place? Use your entrepreneurial endeavors as a force for positive change and work towards building a legacy that extends beyond financial gain.

Networking and Collaboration

As you reflect on your journey, recognize the power of collaboration and networking. The entrepreneurial ecosystem thrives on connections. Nurture a healthy relationship with fellow business owners, mentors, and possible partners. These connections can provide insights, support, and opportunities you might not find on your own.

Continuous Innovation

Innovation is the lifeblood of entrepreneurship. Be relentless in your pursuit of new ideas, better solutions, and improved processes. Encourage creativity within your team; never settle for the status quo. Remember, even industry giants can be disrupted by innovative startups.

The Entrepreneur's Mindset

Ultimately, success in entrepreneurship is not just about what you do but how you think. Cultivate the entrepreneurial mindset - one that embraces uncertainty values resilience, and thrives on creativity. This mindset will be your compass as you navigate the ever-evolving landscape of entrepreneurship.

Your entrepreneurial journey is not ending; it's evolving. Embrace the fluidity of this path, celebrate your victories, and learn from your defeats. Stay committed to personal growth, adapt to change, and continue to innovate.

As you do, you'll not only achieve success in your endeavors but also contribute to the dynamic tapestry of entrepreneurship that shapes our world. Your journey is a testament to the human spirit's ability to create, adapt, and inspire.

Now, go forth and write the next chapter of your entrepreneurial story with confidence and determination.